2006

D0606637

Humpback

IMAGES OF HAWAI'I'S WHALES

Mutual Publishing

Copyright © 2006 by Mutual Publishing, LLC

No part of this book may be reproduced in any form or by any electronic or mechanical means, including information storage and retrieval devices or systems, without prior written permission from the publisher, except that brief passages may be quoted for reviews.

All rights reserved

All images courtesy of SeaPics.com

ISBN-10: 1-56647-760-3
ISBN-13: 978-1-56647-760-4
Library of Congress Catalog Card Number: 2005936543

First Printing, February 2006
Second Printing, June 2007
Third Printing, August 2014

Mutual Publishing, LLC
1215 Center Street, Suite 210
Honolulu, Hawai'i 96816
Ph: 808-732-1709 / Fax: 808-734-4094
email: info@mutualpublishing.com
www.mutualpublishing.com

Printed in South Korea

INTRODUCTION

In the ancient Hawaiian chant of creation called the Kumulipo, the ocean, land, and all of its creatures were formed out of coral. All fish creatures were assigned to be a guardian of a land plant. The largest of the fish, the koholā, or whale, was chosen as the guardian of the ʻiliahi, or sandalwood tree. Sadly, both the sandalwood tree and the whale eventually became valued commodities of human consumption, plundered almost to the point of extinction.

Today, many species of whales, including the humpback, are still considered endangered. Scientists estimate that the pre-whaling population of humpbacks (counted before the early nineteenth century) was about 15,000. The current count is about less than half that number, signifying not only a considerable dwindling but also the challenge of repopulation.

As many as 5,000 to 6,000 humpback whales migrate to Hawaiʻi every winter. They spend most of the year in Alaskan waters, feeding to prepare for the long migration south to these winter breeding grounds. Usually arriving in December but sometimes as early as November, they roam throughout the Hawaiian Island chain with the highest concentration of whales found around Maui, Molokaʻi, Lānaʻi, Kahoʻolawe, and a shallow area between Molokaʻi and Lānaʻi known as Penguin Banks.

All of the images included here (except for page 4) are of humpbacks in Hawaiʻi. As one of nature's most exquisite sea animals, the humpback has adapted over centuries to live a wondrous life cycle that includes instinctively swimming across all the earth's oceans. The humpback continues to beguile and bewilder humans, yet it is exactly the humpback's mysterious nature that inspires the admiration and awe we feel.

© Duncan Murrell / SeaPics.com

These humpback whales, spouting as high as twenty or thirty feet in the air,
begin their journey towards the warm waters of Hawai'i from Alaska around October,
swimming at a steady pace of three to eight miles per hour.

Humpbacks arrive in Hawai'i's waters by December. Here, an adult humpback whale surfaces in West Maui beneath a rainbow.

© Michael S. Nolan / SeaPics.com

© Michael S. Nolan / SeaPics.com

Whale watching has become a favorite activity for both visitors and kamaʻāina (residents). The humpback whale is one of the most fascinating sea mammals to witness, observe, and study.

Among whales, the humpback is considered medium-sized, averaging forty-five feet in body length and weighing about forty to forty-five tons. An adult humpback has a dark gray to black body with occasional white splotches.

© James D. Watt / SeaPics.com

© Masa Ushioda / SeaPics.com

The humpback is named for the humped appearance of its arch when diving or surfacing. A humpback's dorsal fin is small, although its shape and size varies by individual whale. Scars also uniquely mark each humpback's dorsal fin.

Barnacles attach themselves to many parts of the whale, including at the end of pectoral fins, or flippers. When barnacles fall off, they usually leave a white ring of scar tissue.

© James D. Watt / SeaPics.com

© Masa Ushioda / SeaPics.com

The longest of any cetacean, its pectoral fins measure about one-third of a humpback's body size. *Megaptera novaeangliae*, the humpback's scientific name, means "great wings of New England."

© Masa Ushioda / SeaPics.com

Parasitic acorn barnacles cluster under the chin of a humpback. Barnacles generally fall off from a whale when it arrives in the warmer waters of Hawai'i.

© Masa Ushioda / SeaPics.com

Considered a baleen whale, the humpback has an expandable, pleated throat that enables it to gulp more than 500 gallons of water and food at one time. The baleen, comprised of keratin structures much like human fingernails, strains food from the water, nearly one ton per day.

© Doug Perrine / HWRF / SeaPics.com only for uses that are educational or promote awareness & conservation of marine mammals / Photo was taken under NMFS research permit #587.

The humpback's tail is a powerful body part that drives the whale through its long migrations. Complete with a fin, or flukes, it grows to fifteen feet. A humpback's flukes feature black and white patterns and is uniquely shaped with serrated edges. This humpback diving in Kona waters exhibits orca tooth scars on its flukes.

© Masa Ushioda / SeaPics.com

The humpback breathes voluntarily, coming up for air. When the humpback exhales, water erupts from its two blowholes, creating a spout that can reach as high as thirty feet.

The graceful arch of a breaching humpback never ceases to awe all who serendipitously witness this acrobatic display. Why whales breach, or soar out of the water, still remains a mystery. Researchers speculate that it is a form of communication for whales.

© James D. Watt / SeaPics.com

A pair of humpback whales creates a postcard moment with a double breach.

© James D. Watt / SeaPics.com

© James D. Watt / SeaPics.com

Another distinctive behavior of the humpback is the spy hop, when it slowly rises straight up and maintains its head above water, exposing its eyes. Spy hopping also involves a vertical 90- to 180-degree turn before disappearing into the water. Here, two humpbacks engage in a double spy hop.

© Masa Ushioda / SeaPics.com

A humpback often extends one or both of its pectoral fins and slaps them against the water, either once or multiple times. Pec slapping and waving are not considered an aggressive form of behavior.

A whale's tail is so powerful that it takes only one or two thrusts to breach.

© Masa Ushioda / SeaPics.com

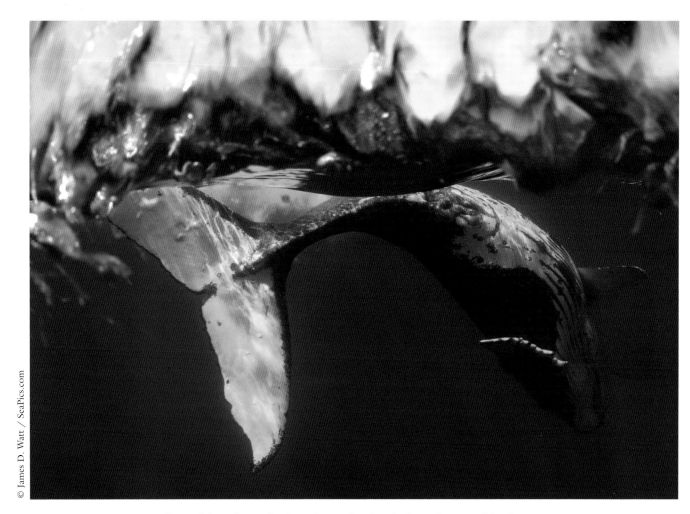

© James D. Watt / SeaPics.com

Graceful and acrobatic, a humpback whale swims upside down.

© Masa Ushioda / SeaPics.com

A humpback also uses its tail in specific forms of behavior. An explosive sound generally follows a tail slap, when a humpback forcefully slaps its flukes while maintaining its balance underwater.

© Michael S. Nolan / SeaPics.com

A humpback can also perform an inverted tail lob, as exemplified by this whale in the ʻAuʻau Channel near Maui.

Tail extension is a behavior in which a whale holds its tail above the surface for extended periods of time, which can sometimes be as long as four hours.

© Masa Ushioda / SeaPics.com

© Masa Ushioda / SeaPics.com

Face to face with a videographer, a humpback creates a bubble trail from its blowholes.

© James D. Watt / SeaPics.com

Adult pairs are common on breeding and feeding grounds. Male-female pairs are relatively stable, lasting from several hours to a day or longer. These pairs may lead to the formation of competitive groups, where other males challenge the primary male for his place with the female.

© Masa Ushioda / SeaPics.com

In a competitive group, two males may engage in a fight, or aggressive behavior, to gain access to a potential mate.

During courtship, a male humpback whale will boldly lunge towards a female to attract her attention.

© Masa Ushioda / SeaPics.com

© Masa Ushioda / SeaPics.com

On breeding grounds, male humpbacks compete against each other for a potential mate. The head lunge, when a humpback charges forward with most of its head surfacing out of the water, is considered one type of competitive behavior.

© Doug Perrine / HWRF / SeaPics.com only for uses that are educational or promote awareness & conservation of marine mammals / Photo was taken under NMFS research permit #587.

Sometimes you can hear a humpback open and close its jaws in a loud clap. The jaw clap is another form of competitive male behavior. Here, a male humpback observed in a competitive group in Kona exhibits lunge, jaw clap, and chin slap.

© James D. Watt / SeaPics.com

Singing is one of the most intriguing whale behaviors displayed by the male humpback. Theories of why a whale sings include courting to social communication and interaction between males. Generally, a singer hangs upside down while submerged and stationary, but sometimes a whale may sing while traveling.

© Masa Ushioda / SeaPics.com

Blowing bubbles is another behavior a male humpback may display to court
a female when approaching her.

© Doug Perrine / HWRF / SeaPics.com only for uses that are educational or promote awareness & conservation of marine mammals / Photo was taken under NMFS research permit #587.

Two humpback whales in courtship underwater. The female swims in front of the male, its hemispherical lobe visible on her tail.

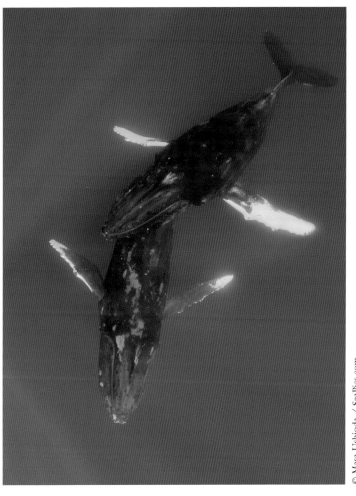

© Masa Ushioda / SeaPics.com

The male humpback gently glides over the female to complete the courtship and mating ritual.

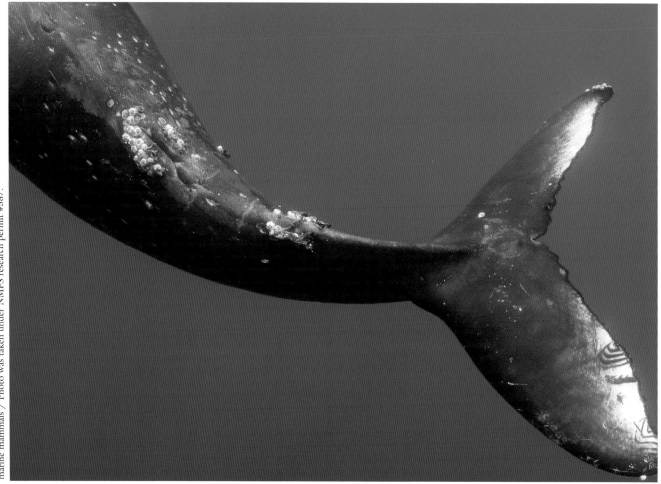

© Doug Perrine / HVRF / SeaPics.com only for uses that are educational or promote awareness & conservation of marine mammals / Photo was taken under NMFS research permit #587.

The genital and mammary slits, hemispherical lobe, and anal opening are located externally on the tail of a female humpback. Note the barnacles around the genitals and the orca tooth rakes on the flukes.

© James D. Watt / SeaPics.com

After a gestation period of about ten to twelve months, a calf is born, generally in Hawaiian waters, as humpbacks migrate to the Islands to mate and rear their young.

© Jon Cornforth / SeaPics.com

A humpback calf and its mother remain in near-shore waters for about a week after the birth.

A calf always swims close to its mother during the first months of life, even maintaining physical contact. Approximately measuring twelve feet long and weighing two tons, a calf usually doubles in size after one year.

© James D. Watt / SeaPics.com

© Masa Ushioda / SeaPics.com

After conception, the father does not associate with the pregnant female, and she is left on her own to give birth. After the birth, a different male, called an escort, joins the female and calf with the intent to mate with the female when she enters estrus again. The escort also provides protection for the mother and calf, if necessary.

© Doug Perrine / HWRF / SeaPics.com / Photo was taken under National Marine Fisheries (NMFS) scientific research permit #882 issued to Hawaii Whale Research Foundation (HWRF).

Competition exists even for the escort. This escort on the right uses his fluke to ward off a male challenger approaching from behind.

Growing calves are a curious bunch, often playful like this one that blows a trail of bubbles underwater in the 'Au'au Channel near Maui.

© Michael S. Nolan / SeaPics.com

A mother whale and her calf surface together off the Maui coast. Calves surface more frequently than adult whales, about every three to five minutes compared to adults who breathe every ten to fifteen minutes.

© Michael S. Nolan / SeaPics.com

© Michael S. Nolan / SeaPics.com

A calf will nurse during its first year of life, weaning off when it returns to the feeding grounds of Alaskan waters where it will start to ingest small fish and euphausiids.

Sometimes, a whale is sighted from afar off various shores, especially on Maui.

© Masa Ushioda / SeaPics.com

© James D. Watt / SeaPics.com

A spy hopping humpback playfully surprises a boat of local fishermen. As humpbacks are a protected species, federal guidelines require a viewing distance of at least 100 yards in the ocean.

Lone whales tend to be male adults, sub-adults (not yet physically mature), or yearlings (recently weaned calves).

© Masa Ushioda / SeaPics.com

© Michael S. Nolan / SeaPics.com

In the early spring, the first wave of humpback whales returns to their feeding grounds, where their lives will be centered around a continual search for food to prepare for the next season of migration back to their breeding grounds of Hawai'i.

Humpback whales dive in synchronicity with friendly flukes in the air.

© Masa Ushioda / SeaPics.com

A humpback takes a breath upon emerging from the water at sunset.

© Masa Ushioda / SeaPics.com